STAMP
Your Stuff

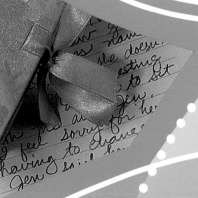

MaryJo McGraw

North Light Books
Cincinnati, Ohio
www.artistsnetwork.com

08 07 06 05 04   5 4 3 2 1

Library of Congress Cataloging-in-Publication Division
McGraw, MaryJo

  Stamp your stuff/ MaryJo McGraw

   p. cm.

   Summary: Provides instructions for using stamps, paints, and other materials to decorate everyday objects and show off one's personal style.

   ISBN 1-58180-386-9 (alk. paper)

    1. Rubber stamp printing—Juvenile literature. [1. Rubber stamp printing. 2. Handicraft.] I. Title.

TT867.M38 2004

761—dc22   2003054047

Editor: David Oeters

Designer: Lisa Buchanan

Layout Artist: Camillia De Rhodes

Production Coordinator: Sara Dumford

Photographer: Christine Polomsky

ABOUT THE AUTHOR

MaryJo McGraw is a nationally known rubber stamp artist and author whose work has been featured in leading rubber stamp enthusiast publications. Innovative techniques and creative teaching methods have made her a much sought-after instructor at conventions, retreats, cruises and stores for over fifteen years. She is the author of six North Light rubber stamping books, including *Making Greeting Cards with Creative Material*, *Creative Rubber Stamping Techniques* and *Greeting Card Magic with Rubber Stamps*.

Metric Conversion Chart

TO CONVERT	TO	MULTIPLY BY
Inches	Centimeters	2.54
Centimeters	Inches	0.4
Feet	Centimeters	30.5
Centimeters	Feet	0.03
Yards	Meters	0.9
Meters	Yards	1.1
Sq. Inches	Sq. Centimeters	6.45
Sq. Centimeters	Sq. Inches	0.16
Sq. Feet	Sq. Meters	0.09
Sq. Meters	Sq. Feet	10.8
Sq. Yards	Sq. Meters	0.8
Sq. Meters	Sq. Yards	1.2
Pounds	Kilograms	0.45
Kilograms	Pounds	2.2
Ounces	Grams	28.4
Grams	Ounces	0.04

DEDICATION

For all my girls especially Trisha, Tori, Brook and Chelsea. The <u>next</u> one is for you Drew!

ACKNOWLEDGMENTS

Thanks again to my friends at North Light especially Tricia Waddell for cheering me on and Christine (do it for the kids) Polomsky for all the laughs!

Last, but not least, I owe a huge debt of gratitude to David Oeters for his tireless work on this book. Thanks David!

Table of contents

Introduction p.6
Materials p.8
Basic Techniques p.10
Making Stamps p.12
Eraser Stamps p.12
Foam Stamps p.13
Punch Stamps p.14
Clay Stamps p.16
Resources p.63

PROJECTS p.18

Computer Disk Journal p.26

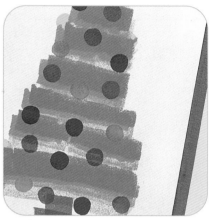

Holiday Greetings Card p.32

Paper Bead Bracelet p.20

Angel Picture Frame p.30

Bulletin Board p.36
Clay Pins, Bulletin Board Hooks p.38–39

Hand On Heart Friendship Card p.24

Butterfly Tote Bag p.40

CD Journal p.48
Making Handmade Paper p.48
Making the CD Case Journal p.51

Treasure Box p.56
Game Box p.59

Birthday Tag Card p.42

Silvery Valentine's Day Card p.54

Thank You Card p.60

Flowered Lamp p.44
Terra-Cotta Desk Pots p.47

STAMP your stuff!

Stamping your stuff is more than just stamping some stuff. It's your stuff! Your room is much more than just a place to sleep. You read there, hang out with friends, talk on the phone and lay around and dream.

Everyone likes to have their own space, and today it is easier than ever to decorate it just the way you like it!

This book will show you how to use stamps, paints and simple, everyday materials you can buy in your local craft store to add style and personality to the everyday stuff in your life. You'll learn how to prepare a surface for stamping, how to add cool extras like beads, ribbons and yarn.

This book will give you tons of great ideas for making your stuff a true reflection of you.

Pick a theme. Make it something you love like animals, hippie chic or nature. Choose a few stamps that fit your theme and you can do a whole room in your own special style.

Be proud to show off your style in the everyday things you use!

Before you get started stamping your stuff, you'll need to pick up some supplies. Just about everything in this book can be found in craft stores. If there is something you have trouble finding, just ask a clerk and they should be able to help you.

Rubber Stamps

No matter what kind of rubber stamp you have, there are generally three parts: the mount, the cushion and the die. The **mount** is where you hold the stamp, and can be made of wood or other materials. The **cushion** is usually made of foam and helps make a good image when you press down. The **die** is the most important part because it transfers the image to the project. There are many types of stamp designs and types of stamps, but they all do the same thing: transfer an image.

Inks

There are three basic ink types: dye, pigment and solvent. **Dye-based** pads are the types you see lying around the house or office and are water-soluble, so they are easy to clean and are less likely to stain. **Pigment** inks absorb into the paper and are good for cool effects, but won't work on all papers or surfaces. **Solvent-based** inks are used for stamping on unusual surfaces and won't smear like dyes, but they can definitely stain your clothes. I suggest getting black in all three ink forms, and then a variety of other colors.

Paints and Primers

Acrylic paint sticks to many surfaces, especially if the surface has been correctly prepared. Most of the projects in this book use acrylic craft paints, which clean up with water and are available at craft stores. You can substitute **poster paint** for porous surfaces like bulletin boards and picture frames, but it doesn't last as well. **Gesso** is a primer that makes a surface better for acrylic paint. After it is dry you will notice that it feels chalky, which is perfect for the paint. Some of the projects in this book have been primed using gesso, and some not. If you have a project and are not sure if you should prime it, then just prime it!

Glue

Liquid white glue (school glue) is fine for many of the projects in this book and works on lots of surfaces, especially if the glue is covered by paper, glitter or some kind of other decoration. When you use a wet glue on paper, use a brush to spread thin a small amount of the glue to keep the paper from buckling. Solid **glue sticks** are excellent for paper to paper projects like card layering. Whichever glue you use, start slowly by adding a little at a time. A **clear glaze**, like Diamond Glaze, is a dimensional adhesive because it dries to a clear, glasslike finish and securely holds many mediums. You can brush it on for a super-shiny look as well.

Pencils and Pens

Always keep a **pencil** on hand for projects. They are excellent for free-hand drawing designs and lines, and the eraser tip can be a quick embellishment stamp. **Decorative pens** come in many varieties, such as water-based and oil-based, fluorescent and metallic, and in many styles and colors. They are simple to use and look fantastic. Always do a test spot to make sure the pen will work on your surface. **Gel pens** are great on paper, and some even work on fabric. I use them to highlight the outline of a stamped image, which adds cool detail to a plain design.

Scissors

You will need a good pair of scissors for many of the projects in this book. Paper can dull scissors, so it is a good idea to have a pair for paper, and a pair for other stuff like ribbon and fabric. **Decorative edger scissors** have blades that make a cool pattern with each cut. They are useful for adding a bit of style to your paper projects. You can find them at craft and scrapbook stores.

Basic techniques

TIP

While you do the stamping, you may need another person to help hold the object you are stamping—especially when you are stamping curved surfaces.

Stamping is easy and fun. Once you have a few basic stamping skills, you can use them for so many different projects. Here are a few basic techniques you should know before you start stamping your stuff.

BASIC STAMPING

The secret to making a good stamp is preparing the stamp and the paper first, then using a smooth motion to apply the stamp. This method is for using acrylic paint, but the basic ideas work for inks as well.

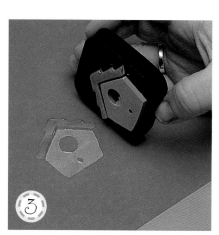

1

APPLY THE PAINT
Use a brush to apply paint to a stamp. On a new stamp it is a good idea to apply a single thin layer of paint to the stamp and let it dry. When you are ready to stamp, this layer will help hold paint and make a better stamped image.

2

CLEAN THE STAMP
If you have excess paint on your stamp, your stamp won't make good images. Use an old soapy toothbrush or paintbrush to remove any excess paint from your stamps before you use them. Wipe off the residue with a damp washcloth.

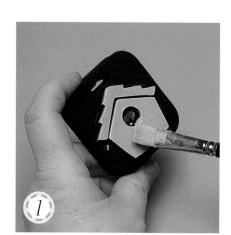

3

STAMP THE SURFACE
On flat surfaces like paper, apply the stamp to the surface, pressing evenly on the top of the stamp.

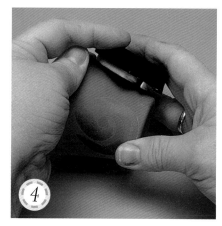

4

STAMPING A CURVED SURFACE
To stamp on curved surfaces, roll the stamp slowly, making sure all the edges touch the surface.

CLEANING YOUR STAMPS

It's important to clean your stamps when you are done using them. A stamp that is full of crusty old paint and sticky ink never makes a pretty image.

CLEANING A STAMP
Use a damp paper towel or a baby wipe to blot off the ink and paint. Use a wet paintbrush to dig old paint and ink from the cut-out areas of the stamp. When finished, make sure the stamp surface is clean and not sticky.

TIP

There are cleaners made especially for stamps. They have a scrubby top for easy cleaning.

TIP

Glue sticks are great for clean gluing jobs. For jobs that need stickier glue, use white glue. If you use white glue on paper, use just a small amount and apply it with a toothpick for a clean result.

GLUING CARDS

Gluing paper can be a lot trickier than you think! Nothing is worse than making a perfect image, only to glue it crooked on the front of a card. Here are a few tips for perfect glue jobs.

APPLY THE GLUE
Apply your glue stick to the back of the paper and make sure the glue goes all the way to the edge, so there is glue everywhere.

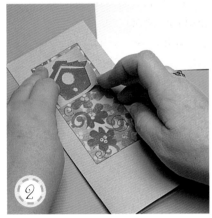

ADJUST THE PAPER
First adjust the paper on the surface of the card without pressing down. Make sure it is straight and then press it in place.

MAKING
stamps

Stuff you'll need
✓ paper   ✓ ink
✓ eraser   ✓ scissors *(optional)*

Just because you can't find the perfect stamp design doesn't mean you have to give up! Making stamps is simple! When you look for things that can make a good stamp, find materials that soak up ink or paint. Sponges, foam and other squishy items that hold a shape are great.

ERASER STAMPS

Look around your house—I bet you have several different shaped erasers that could be great stamps! It is easy to find stars and hearts or even cars and flowers stamps. All of these shapes can be stamps.

INK THE ERASER
Put ink or paint on one side of the eraser. This will be the side you stamp. If you like, use scissors to carefully cut a stamping design out of a large eraser.

STAMP THE PAPER
Press the eraser onto the paper.

TIP

When you are creating a background of shapes on a piece of paper as we have done here, start the design half way off the paper. Just be sure you have scrap paper underneath!

FOAM STAMPS

Here is a simple way to make a stamp in any shape you like using just some glue, a foam pad, a block and scissors!

Stuff you'll need

- ✓ foam sheets or thin packing foam
- ✓ block of wood or recycled box
- ✓ heart pattern
- ✓ marker or pen
- ✓ scissors
- ✓ white glue

TIP

Foam sheets are available at craft stores. Just ask a clerk if you are having trouble finding them.

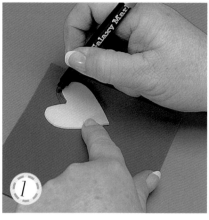

DRAW THE DESIGN
Trace the pattern or draw the design you want to stamp onto the foam with a marker or pen. Make sure the design is no bigger than your block.

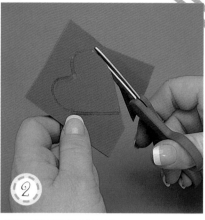

CUT OUT THE SHAPE
Use scissors to carefully cut the design from the foam.

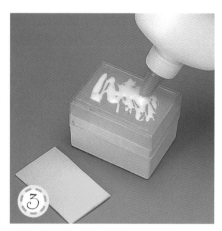

ADD GLUE
Cut another piece of foam to fit on your block. This will be a cushion for your stamp. Add glue to one side of your block, then glue the cushion onto the block.

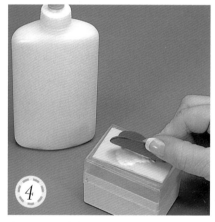

GLUE THE STAMP
Add your shape to the cushion with more glue. Let it dry before you use it.

TIP

You could practice drawing the design first on a piece of paper before drawing on the foam.

PUNCH STAMPS

Punches come in all different shapes and sizes. Most are available through craft and discount stores. Scrapbook stores usually have a fantastic supply of paper punches. For this type of stamp you will be punching through foam with a paper punch. Most foam sheets will fit through the punch, as will many kinds of recycled packing foam and even some thin sponges.

Stuff you'll need

✓ foam sheet
✓ handle, box or block
✓ paper punch
✓ paintbrush
✓ white glue

LINE UP YOUR PUNCH
It is easier to see where to punch by turning the punch upside down. Do this to make sure your punch is lined up.

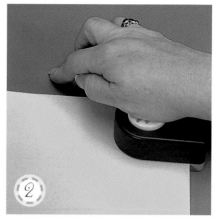

PUNCH THE DESIGN
Place the foam and the punch on a sturdy surface and press hard.

PUNCH A SECOND SHAPE
If the shape has a lot of detail, like this dragonfly, punch out 2 shapes. The two shapes will give you a better stamp.

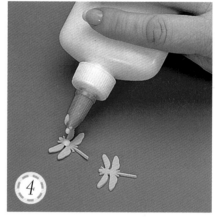

APPLY GLUE
Spread glue on one side of one of the shapes. If the shapes are small, don't use too much glue. Just a drop will do.

TIP

If your punch is stiff, you can sharpen it by punching through aluminum foil. If your punch gets stuck, whack the side of it to loosen the material.

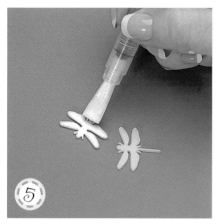

⑤

SPREAD THE GLUE
Use a paintbrush to carefully spread the glue on the design. This will keep the glue even on the foam.

⑥

GLUE THE FIGURES TOGETHER
Lay the shapes on top of each other. Make sure they are even and no edges are sticking out. Then smooth them together carefully.

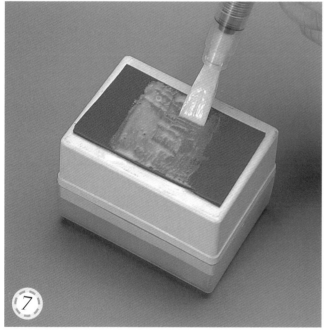

⑦

GLUE ON THE CUSHION
Add another layer of foam to your handle or box. Apply glue to the stamp area with a paintbrush.

⑧

GLUE THE STAMP
Use glue to attach the stamp to the cushion. Let dry for an hour before using the new stamp.

CLAY STAMPS

There are many kinds of clay out there that are made especially for kids. The clays you can use to make stamps stay a little soft even when they are dry. A good hint for buying clay is to look for the word "foam." If it has "foam" anywhere in the name or on the package, it should work.

Stuff you'll need

- ✓ air-dry clay
- ✓ small cookie cutters
- ✓ drinking glass
- ✓ plastic knife
- ✓ white glue

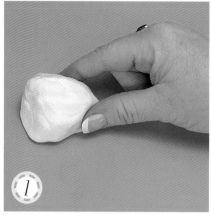

①

PREPARE THE CLAY

You need a hunk of clay big enough to fit in your hand. Roll and squeeze it in your hand until it is soft.

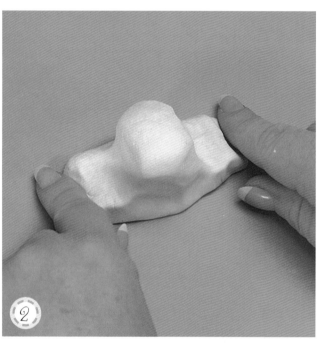

②

SHAPE THE STAMP

Use your hands to form the clay into the shape of a handle. Make one side very flat. This is the side the stamp shape will be on. The other side should have a bump that you can hold on to when you are stamping. Trim the excess clay with a plastic knife. Set the clay aside to dry overnight.

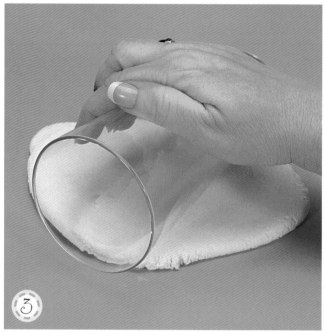

③

ROLL THE CLAY

Take another hunk of clay and flatten it like a pancake. Roll over it with the side of a glass to make it very smooth.

TIP

You can make block-like handles by cutting large squares of clay with a plastic knife.

CUT YOUR SHAPES
Use a cookie cutter to cut out differ-ent shapes from the flattened clay.

LET SHAPES DRY
Be sure each stamp you make will fit the handle! Let the shapes dry overnight, or follow the directions on the clay.

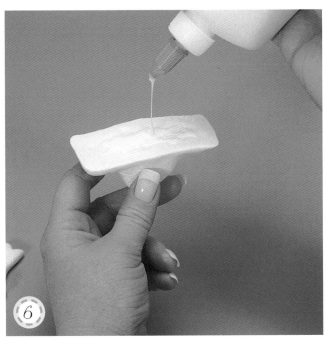

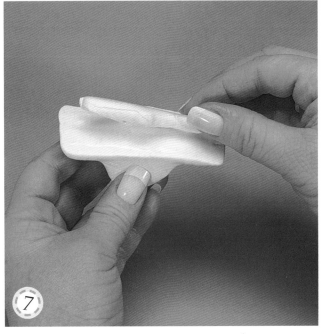

GLUE THE HANDLE
After the clay is dry, apply glue to the flat bottom of the handle. Don't use too much glue or it will ooze from the sides.

ADD THE STAMP
Press the stamp design to the glue on the handle. Make sure the stamp is centered. Let dry for an hour before making your first stamp.

GeT stamping!

Okay, you know how to make stamps, and you have an idea about how to use them. Now is the time to put it all together. It's time to make some stuff!

In the next few pages I'm going to show you how to make a few things, but once you get started stamping you'll see there is so much more you can do.

What about gifts? Many of the projects in this book make excellent gifts, and everyone loves to receive something handmade. It makes a personal statement because you spent your time creating something special for someone special to you. Give a gift you would love to get, like a cool bracelet, a tiny book, a beautiful picture frame or a secret journal. Make one for yourself and give one to your best friend, your mom or your aunt.

Make something more special by finding out what your family and friends love. Ask questions and uncover their favorite colors or images. Do they like angels, horses, fairies, or perhaps nature and ladybugs?

STAMPING ADVENTURE

In this book are a variety of projects and styles that are simple to change to suit your mood and personal theme. A flowery lamp could be done in stars and moons for a celestial look, or a smiley face for a '60s retro room!

Look around the house for throw-away items you can decorate and reuse, like small boxes or cans that can be used to hold pens, scissors or hair stuff. Yard sales are great places to find cool stuff that's cheap, like old bulletin boards and picture frames. Most craft stores have plenty of foam stamps for decorating, and some are under two dollars! Just keep your eyes open.

The stamping adventure possibilities are everywhere, and your stuff will never be the same.

PAPER
bead bracelet

Paper beads are fun to make. You can use scrap papers from junk mail and even old gift wrap. Making the beads is an easy project you can work on even while watching TV. This bracelet is so pretty, your friends will beg you to make one for them.

You can make tons of other great stuff with these beads. Decorate hair bands or string a bunch together and wrap them around curtains for tiebacks.

① COLOR THE PAPER
Protect your work surface with scrap paper or an old newspaper. Rub an ink pad over the surface of the lightweight paper. Use several ink colors to make a pretty pattern.

② BUFF THE INK
While the paper is wet with the ink, use a paper towel to buff the ink (wipe it off). This will blend the colors together and remove excess ink.

STAMP THE PAPER

Use a darker ink to stamp a pattern over the paper. Choose any stamp design you like.

CUT THE TRIANGLES

Cut out 11 long skinny triangles from the colored paper. The triangles should be about 4" (10cm) tall and ¾" (2cm) at the bottom.

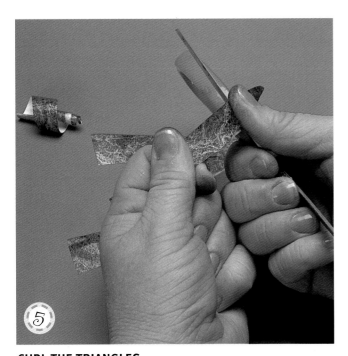

CURL THE TRIANGLES

Run scissors over the triangles to curl them. Then roll the strips beginning at the fat end and ending with the point of the triangle. Make sure the rolls are tight.

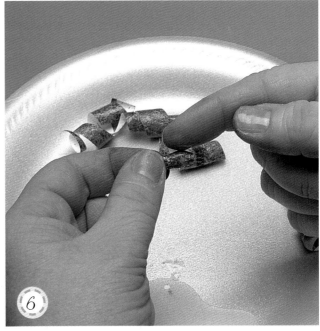

GLUE THE TRIANGLE

Take the rolled triangle, which is now bead shaped, and seal it with clear glue. Roll the bead in the glue so it is completely covered.

TIP

Keep glitter under control by using an old shirt box. Put the item you are applying glitter to in the box, then apply the glue and sprinkle glitter. When you are done, shake the glitter down to a corner of the box and carefully return the extra glitter to the bottle or plastic bag.

(7)

ADD GLITTER

While the bead is still wet with the glue, roll it in glitter. Do this for all the beads. Make sure all the beads are dry before continuing.

(8)

ADD BEADS TO THE ELASTIC BAND

Begin by wrapping the jewelry band four times loosely around your wrist and cut. To this length of cord add a normal bead, then add one paper bead, then another normal bead to the band. You will have a paper bead between two normal beads.

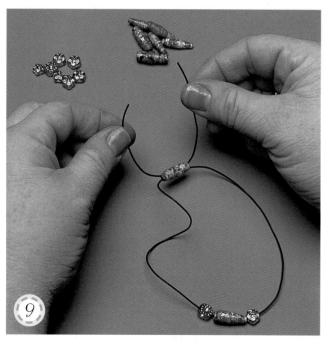

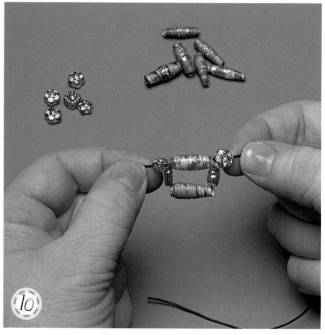

(9)

ADD ANOTHER PAPER BEAD

Add another paper bead. Draw both ends of the jewelry band through the paper bead. Pull the string tight. This is known as the ladder bracelet method.

(10)

CONTINUE BEADING

Add another bead to both ends of the jewelry bands, placing them on either side of the paper bead. Add beads as you did in steps 8 through 10 to complete the bracelet. You will probably need at least eleven paper beads on the string.

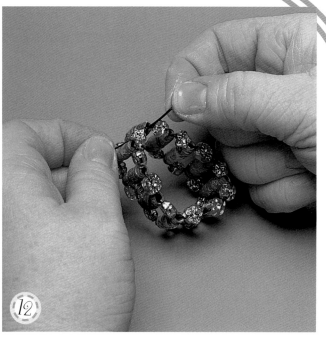

CLOSE THE BRACELET

When you have all the beads on the jewelry band, make sure you've left a little room at the end of the elastic band. Then take the longest side of the elastic and pull it through the very first bead.

TIE A KNOT

Tie a square knot into the bracelet to secure the beads. In tying off the bracelet you might need a helping hand, so don't be afraid to ask a friend for help.

DIFFERENT COLORS, DIFFERENT STAMPS, DIFFERENT BRACELETS!

Just a change in paper color, or a different ink, or trying a new stamp will create a totally different look for your bracelet! What design do you want for your own bracelet?

TIP

A square knot is right over left, then left over right. It should look like two connected loops in the string.

HAND ON HEART
friendship card

Good friends are important. When you need a quick card for a thank you or just a special note, this handmade card is perfect! It's an excellent way to tell someone special how much they mean to you, and a good reminder of what it means to be a true friend. Make several of them, so you don't forget anyone you care about.

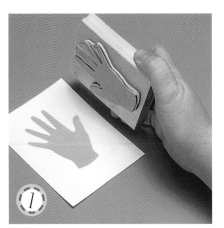

STAMP THE HAND

Cut a piece of light-colored cardstock smaller than the front of your card. Stamp the image of the hand on the light-colored cardstock. Make sure the stamp isn't too big or small for the card.

MORE IDEAS

This would be a great card in pinks (hand) and purples (heart). Add just a bit of glam by creating a border with a line of white glue and then sprinkling on glitter.

STAMP THE HEART

Wait until the hand dries, then stamp the heart in the middle of the hand in a darker color.

TRIM THE CARD

Trim the card with the scissors using a wavy cut. You could use decorative scalloped scissors as well. Make sure you don't cut your stamped images.

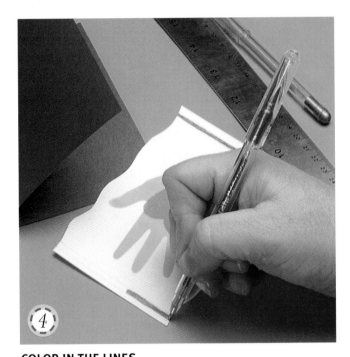

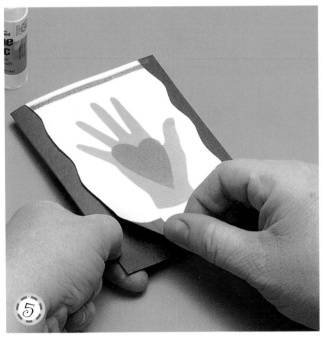

COLOR IN THE LINES

Use a straightedge and the gel pen to color decorative lines on the top and bottom of the card.

GLUE THE CARD TOGETHER

Glue the light-colored paper to the front of the blue cardstock.

COMPUTER
disk journal

A journal is a special place to keep all your most private thoughts. You can use a computer as a journal, typing your secrets, but now you can use a computer disk to keep your thoughts without a computer! And with this journal, you can decorate the cover so it says something about who you are. Use up all those old computer disks to create little books or other cool stuff.

PREPARE THE BAG

Cut the paper bag down one of the folds. Cut off the bottom of the bag. This will leave one flat piece of paper. Stamp a cool design on the bag in at least three different colors.

TIP

Ask FIRST before starting this project. There might be something important on those disks!

STAMP DOTS

Use the eraser tip of a pencil to stamp colored dots in the blank spots on the paper.

PREPARE THE COVER

Lay the disks on the back of the paper. The paper should stick out from around the disks by about ½" (1cm). There should also be ½" (1cm) in between the disks. Trim away any excess paper with scissors, then set aside the disks.

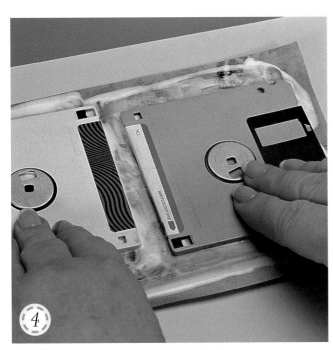

GLUE ON THE DISKS

Spread glue on the back of the paper with a paintbrush, and then glue the disks to their original position on the paper.

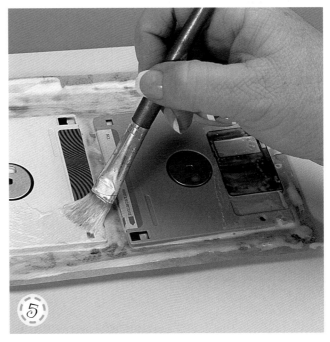

GLUE THE TOP OF THE DISKS

Use the paintbrush to spread extra glue over the top of the disks.

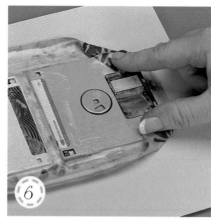

FOLD THE CORNERS

Fold the four corners in and onto the disk. You may need to hold them in place for a few seconds until the glue sticks.

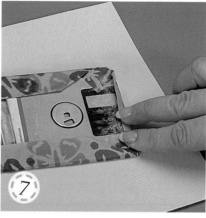

FOLD IN THE SIDES

Fold each of the sides up and over the disks. Press down especially on the corners. You may have to trim away extra paper in the corners.

COVER THE INSIDE

Cut out another piece of brown paper to fit the inside of the book. This piece will cover any of the disks that are still showing. It will be about 7" (18cm) long by 3" (7.6cm) wide. Crumple the paper up into a ball and then smooth it back out.

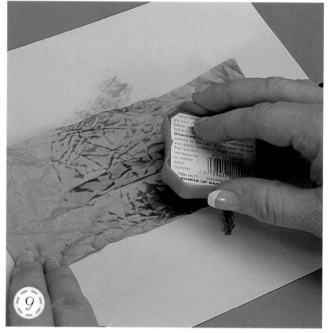

STAMP THE PAPER

Lay the crinkled paper flat on a piece of scrap paper. Rub a stamp pad over the wrinkles on the paper. This will make a cool design. Cover all the edges with color.

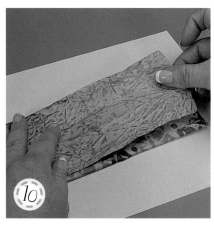

GLUE THE INSIDE COVER
Spread glue over the disks once more. Make sure the glue covers the edges. Lay the wrinkled paper over the glue, then smooth it out with your hands. Set everything out flat to dry.

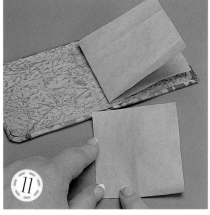

CUT THE PAGES
Create pages for the book by cutting out several more pieces of brown bag. Cut them about 7" (18cm) long by 3" (7.6cm) wide. Fold each piece in half.

TIE THE PAGES
Tie the pages into the book by wrapping the yarn around the fold in the pages and the fold in the book cover.

DRAGONFLY JOURNAL

You can use different colored papers and ink to make your journal. For this journal I used the dragonfly stamp. Glue beads on the cover to make a design that is uniquely yours!

aNGeL
picture frame

Stuff you'll need

- ✓ picture frame
- ✓ heart stamp
- ✓ purple and white acrylic paint
- ✓ craft store angel wings (gold)
- ✓ gold glitter
- ✓ scissors
- ✓ sponge brush
- ✓ hot glue gun
- ✓ clear glaze glue

Add angelic style to your pictures with this fancy frame! This beautiful frame will be a welcome addition to any picture you put on display. This project is so easy, it would be a shame to have a plain frame in your room. Look for wood picture frames with lots of stampable surface. Check out local yard sales and thrift shops with friends and family for cheap old frames.

PAINT THE FRAME
Use a sponge brush to paint the entire frame with purple acrylic paint. Touch up any places where the paint seems thin.

STAMP THE FRAME
Make sure the frame is dry, and then stamp hearts over the front of the frame with white acrylic paint.

ADD GLITTER
Sprinkle glitter on each of the stamped hearts. Do this before the paint dries.

GLUE ON THE WINGS
Cut the angel wings in half and use a glue gun to glue the wings on the back of the frame so they stick out from either side.

MORE IDEAS

All kinds of shapes and sizes of angel wings are available. You can glue them onto more than just picture frames. Mirrors, lamps, bulletin boards and jewelry boxes are just a few other ideas. You can usually find the gold angel wings in a craft store, but if you can't, look for something similar. A golden sun might look neat in the corner!

COVER THE GLITTER
Apply glue over the glitter. Make sure you glue only over the hearts, and not the rest of the frame.

PARTY FRAME

Make this frame the same way as the last one. Paint the frame orange and then stamp swirls and stars. A stream of purple dots completes the party feel! Design your own frame to fit the pictures you decide to display.

HOLIDAY
greetings card

Stuff you'll need

- ✓ white postcard
- ✓ green cardstock
- ✓ candy tin
- ✓ foam or sponge strips
- ✓ inks
- ✓ star stamp
- ✓ yarn
- ✓ doublestick tape
- ✓ scissors
- ✓ pencil
- ✓ white glue

When you start crafting, you'll find you have lots of leftover scraps. Here's a simple idea to make something cool with all those leftovers. With just a few pieces of scrap foam or sponge, you can make a quick tree stamp and card that will brighten anyone's holiday. It's a great card, you've saved some money, and everyone will be proud of you!

CUT THE FOAM
Place a long piece of doublestick tape on a candy tin. Cut foam strips into different sizes, each one should be a little shorter than the last one.

CREATE THE STAMP

Place the longest strip at the bottom, then add a shorter one above it until you get to the top. The stamp should look like a Christmas tree.

STAMP THE CARD

Ink the stamp in green and stamp it in the center of the white postcard.

TIP

There is a lot of stuff you can use as a stamp block, for example, candy tins, scrap pieces of wood and cardboard. You can also buy wooden blocks in your local craft or stamp store.

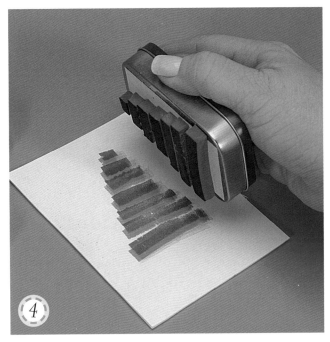

STAMP AGAIN

Stamp the image again on top of the last image. You could use a slightly different colored green, and make the stamp a little crooked from the last one. This makes a fuller looking tree. Continue until the tree looks full, then add a yellow star stamp to the top of the tree.

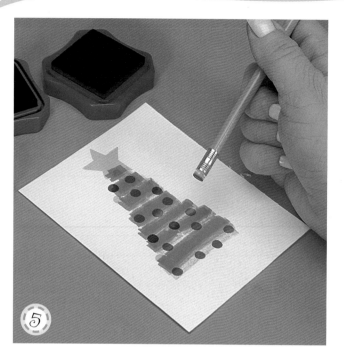

STAMP THE ORNAMENTS

Use the eraser tip of a pencil to stamp colored dots for ornaments. Fill the tree with lots of different colored ornaments.

MAKE THE TREE POT

Cut out the shape of a pot from the foam scraps. Stamp the pot in red at the bottom of the tree.

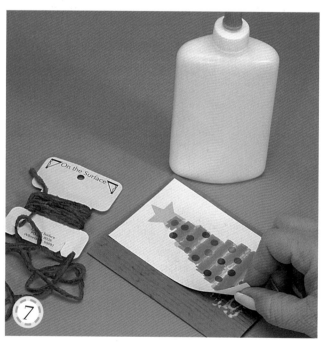

MAKE THE CARD

Trim away some of the extra paper. Glue the white postcard centered to the front of the green card.

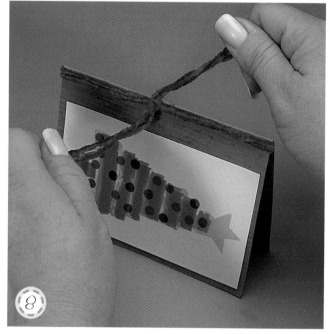

ADD YARN

Tie a piece of yarn around the inside edge of the card, and knot it on the front.

LADYBUG CARD

Here's another super simple card you can make from foam scraps. Stamp a background pattern on a piece of white cardstock. Then make a ladybug- shaped stamp with a piece of leftover foam. Use red and orange ink to stamp a few big ladybugs across the card. Outline the ladybug with a black marker and color its head. Then add dots with a pencil eraser and black ink. Finally, draw in antennae for your ladybug, then glue the paper to the corner of your card. It's that simple!

BULLETIN
board

Stuff you'll need

- ✓ bulletin board
- ✓ map pins
- ✓ flower stamp
- ✓ white, green, pink, light purple and dark purple acrylic paint
- ✓ ribbon
- ✓ paper clay
- ✓ sponge brush
- ✓ round paintbrush
- ✓ craft glue

Who wants a boring brown square bulletin board on the wall? With a bit of paint and stamps you can make your bulletin board a work of art! Stamps make it easy to add perfect flowers to the bulletin board. The results are bright and cheerful, with a splash of color and dash of flowers sure to brighten any room.

PAINT THE BULLETIN BOARD
Basecoat the bulletin board in white using the sponge brush. This may require two coats. Touch up places where the paint seems thin.

PAINT THE STAMP
After the paint dries and you are ready to stamp, apply pink paint to the flower stamp with a paintbrush.

PAINT THE LEAVES
Apply green paint to the leaves of the stamp.

STAMP THE BULLETIN BOARD
Begin by stamping the pink flower. Touch up the paint on your stamp and evenly stamp two rows of pink flowers across the board.

STAMP THE PURPLE FLOWERS
Clean the pink paint from the flower stamp. Apply light purple paint to the flower. Stamp the purple flowers beside the pink flower to make a flower bunch. Make sure the leaves and flowers of the stamps don't touch.

PAINT THE FRAME
Paint the frame in dark purple using the paintbrush. Go over any places where the paint seems thin. Then let it dry.

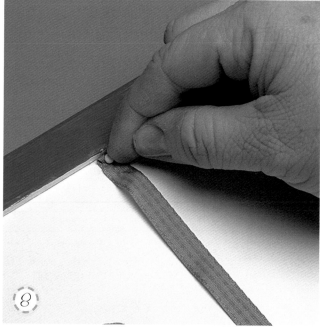

GLUE ON THE RIBBON

Glue the ribbon between the flower bunches you made. Fold the ribbon over at the end, so you can't see the glued area.

SECURE THE RIBBON

Add a map pin to the end of the ribbon, so it will be doubly secure. Repeat steps 7 and 8 with the end of every ribbon on the board.

CLAY PINS

This is a simple way to make great pins for your bulletin board, but they aren't just for bulletin boards. With a little creativity you can find a lot of places a pin can add a bit of personal style.

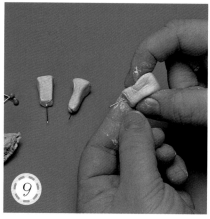

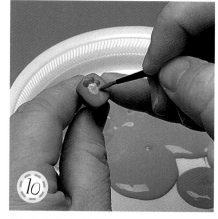

ADD CLAY

Add clay to the top of a map pin. Flatten the clay at the end and shape it around the head of the pin. Leave enough room at the pointy end for the pin to stick in the board. Then let the clay dry.

PAINT THE PINS

Once dry, basecoat the pins in either purple or green. Let the paint dry. Paint a flower on the flat end of the pin using the opposite color (purple for the green pin, and green for the purple pin). Use a round paintbrush to make small dots for the petals. A toothpick would also work.

BULLETIN BOARD HOOKS

For this bulletin board paint the board yellow and stamp colorful images around the border. Swirls, hearts and dots are good stamps to use. Apply the stamps at different angles to make the images more interesting. You can add hooks to the bottom. It's very easy, once you know how.

① MAKE A HOLE
Where you want to add hooks, poke a starter hole in the board with an awl or a similar tool. The end of a paint-brush will work as well.

② SCREW THE HOOKS
Use your fingers to screw cup hooks in the holes.

butterfly
TOTE BaG

Stuff you'll need

- ✓ canvas tote bag
- ✓ butterfly, flowers and bug stamps
- ✓ light blue, purple and aqua acrylic paint
- ✓ textile medium
- ✓ gel pen
- ✓ fluorescent markers
- ✓ paintbrush
- ✓ masking tape

Look around for great stuff you can add fun to with a bit of crafting. Canvas tote bags are everywhere. You can use them for extra purses, or as a book or beach bag. Decorating them to coordinate with your room is getting double duty out of each bag! For this project I added butterflies, flowers and a cool background to a canvas bag.

TAPE THE BAG
Use masking tape to mask off the area of the canvas tote bag you will be painting. It's a good idea to add extra tape to make sure the paint doesn't ooze or leak.

PAINT THE CANVAS BAG
You will need to use either acrylic paint mixed with a textile medium, or fabric paint. First paint around the inside edge of your masking tape, then paint the rest. You might need two coats on the bag. Let the paint dry.

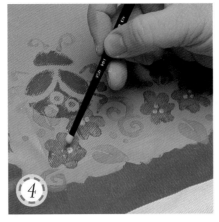

The techniques in this project can be used to stamp many types of fabric, like T-shirts or bandannas.

TIP

Canvas bags are not really meant to be washed, so the paints and pens I used are not all washer safe. I just spot clean the bag or add more stamps over the stains! Mix textile medium with acrylic paint to make it washer safe.

③ STAMP THE BAG

Stamp your images on the canvas bag. Paint the stamp, then stamp the image on the bag. It might help to sketch your design out first so you know where everything will be placed in the picture.

④ FINISH THE STAMPING

Fill the painted area of the canvas bag with stamps and complete the design. You can stamp right to the edge of the painted area as long as you keep the masking tape in place. You can make dots with the end of a paintbrush.

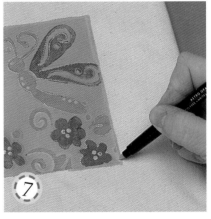

⑤ ADD ACCENTS

Use a gel pen to accent around the stamped images. Fluorescent and fabric markers look fantastic as well.

⑥ ADD A BORDER

Use a fluorescent marker to add a border while the masking tape is still in place. Don't draw over any of the stamped images on the edge, this will make the image look like it is popping off the bag.

⑦ REMOVE THE TAPE

Very carefully remove the tape. Use your pen to add one more little border around the painted square. This will mask any paint bleeding you had under the masking tape.

BIRTHDAY
tag card

Nothing makes a birthday special like a handmade card. This one is pretty enough to make any gift even better! With this project there are a lot of things you can do to personalize the card and make it even more special. Use different kinds of yarn, different stamps or cluster tags together to make a birthday book with stamps, poems or photos.

COLOR THE TAG
Use your ink pad to color the tag yellow.

STAMP THE COLORED TAG
Use a big star stamp in the middle of the tag, then use smaller stamps around it. Use different colored inks for more variety.

LINE THE TAG

Line the outside of the tag with a fluorescent marker.

ADD A TASSEL

Cut several lengths of yarn, each about 6" (15cm). Fold the yarn in half to create a loop. Draw the ends of the yarn through the hole in the tag, and then through the loop. Pull tight.

MORE IDEAS

Look for interesting fibers, like raffia, tassels, ribbon or string. These will add a special look to your card.

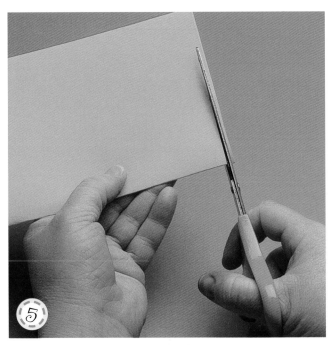

MAKE A CARD

Use a piece of heavy paper or cardstock. Fold it in half, using a straightedge for a crisp crease. When finished, trim the card if needed to make sure the tag fits neatly.

GLUE THE TAG ONTO THE CARD

Use a glue stick and glue the tag onto the front of the card. Make sure you smooth down the edges of the tag.

flowered LaMP

Stuff you'll need

- ✓ lamp with lampshade
- ✓ flower stamp
- ✓ white, green, pink, and purple acrylic or fabric paint
- ✓ textile medium
- ✓ glass and tile medium
- ✓ strip of beads
- ✓ ribbon
- ✓ sponge brush
- ✓ paintbrush
- ✓ flat brush
- ✓ pencil
- ✓ hot glue gun or craft glue
- ✓ varnish

We all have lamps, but how many of us have a lamp with personality? Lamps are made from a lot of different materials like wood, glass and metal.

This project uses ceramic, usually a tough surface to stamp on. You can use these techniques to stamp on most surfaces. Just make sure and check with someone before stamping on a lamp.

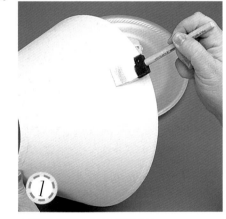

PAINT THE LAMPSHADE

Basecoat the lampshade with white paint and a sponge brush. You'll have to use either textile medium or fabric paint, or the paint won't stick.

STAMP THE LAMPSHADE

Use the flower stamp with green paint for the leaves, and purple and pink for the flowers. You could add some flowers without the leaves for variety. To do this, clean the paint from the leaves and just use the flower part of the stamp.

TOUCH UP THE STAMPS

Because the surface is curved, sometimes the stamp misses. Touch up the stamped images with a paintbrush. Go over any places where the paint seems thin or the stamp missed the fabric.

TIP

If you don't have a glue gun, craft glue will work as well. You might need to use push pins to hold the ribbon on the shade while the glue dries.

ADD ACCENT DOTS

Use an eraser from a pencil to apply dots, and scatter them in the open areas between the flowers.

ADD BEADED RIBBON

Use a glue gun or craft glue to add the strip of beads to the bottom of the lampshade.

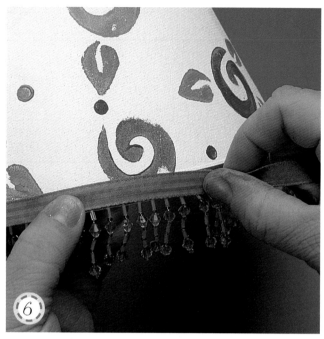

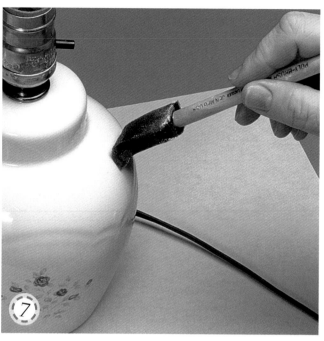

ADD A RIBBON COVER

Glue a colorful ribbon over the top of the bead ribbon. Glue the ribbon on one section at a time and hold it in place while it dries.

PREPARE THE LAMP

Use a sponge brush to paint the lamp base with glass and tile medium, which will prepare the lamp for painting. Allow the medium to dry before continuing.

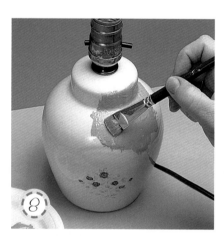

PAINT THE LAMP

Use a flat brush to paint the lamp in purple. It may take several coats.

STAMP THE LAMP

Once the paint is dry, stamp the flowers on the lamp base. You will have to roll the stamp over the lamp carefully. Go over the stamps with a paintbrush to fix any areas the stamp missed.

FINISH THE LAMP

Add accent dots around the flower with the eraser tip of a pencil. To seal the paint, coat it with a varnish when you are finished.

TERRA-COTTA DESK POTS

These pots are a cool way to give some color to a boring desk. They can hold all your desk accessories like rubber bands, paper clips and pens. You can also use them in the bathroom for your hair stuff, cotton balls and swabs. Bigger pots can hold bigger stuff like magazines and plush toys. The terra-cotta pots can be painted pretty much the same way you painted the lamp. These colors are very springlike, but with a little creativity you can choose your own colors.

PAINT THE POTS
Basecoat the pots with acrylic paint. For these pots I used turquoise, pale yellow and pink.

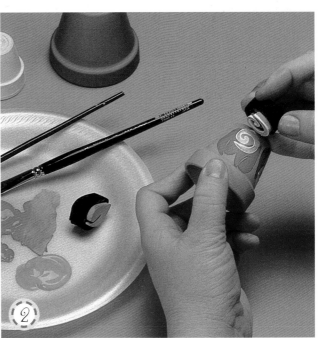

STAMP THE POTS
When the pots are dry, stamp them with designs. Since the pots are small, you can overlap stamps for some wild and crazy designs.

CD journal

This is a simple way to create a beautiful journal from a CD case. This journal uses gorgeous handmade paper that you can make on your own with some simple tools. Handmade paper adds texture and elegance to your projects. With this project, it's also easy to add more pages with a simple bit of origami paper folding. This is an excellent gift for friends that love to write.

Stuff you'll need

✓ CD case
✓ colored construction paper
✓ scrap paper
✓ stamps
✓ inks
✓ ribbon
✓ small water bottle
✓ handmade paper kit (deckle screen, water bucket and board press)
✓ paper towels
✓ scissors
✓ paintbrush
✓ pencil
✓ white glue

MAKING HANDMADE PAPER

The first step to crafting the journal is making handmade paper. This is a lot easier than you might think. You can follow these directions for any project that could use some pretty paper.

TIP

Choose a good variety of paper for the mixture. Magazine inserts work well. So do brown paper bags.

CUT UP THE PAPER

Cut up paper into small chunks (less than ½" [1cm] square). You need a good size pile of paper. Use some light white paper, some thick, rough paper (for texture) as well as a piece or two of paper with color.

FILL THE BOTTLE

Fill the bottle until it's a third of the way full of water, then stuff paper into the bottle.

SHAKE THE BOTTLE

Shake the bottle with the water and paper. Shake it until the paper get pulpy, muddy-like and mushy, without big pockets of water.

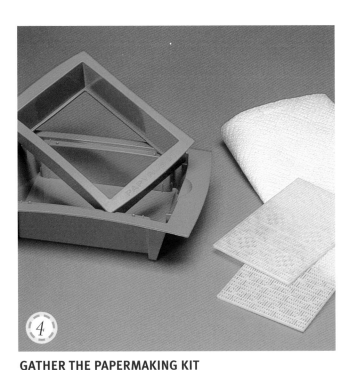

GATHER THE PAPERMAKING KIT

All home papermaking kits should have these parts: a bucket, a frame and a screen for drying. Also gather plenty of absorbent paper towels.

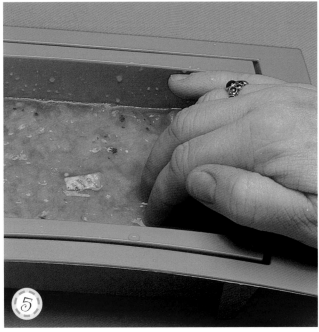

ADD THE PULP

Put the papermaking kit together. Pour the pulpy paper mixture on the screen, which should be in the bucket. Spread the mixture evenly on the screen.

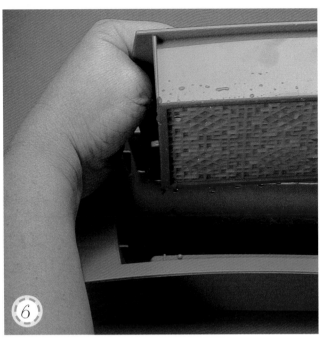

FLATTEN THE PAPER

Put the board on top of the mixture once it is spread evenly. Then pull the screen out of the bucket. Press to squeeze the water out of the mixture and flatten the paper pulp.

REMOVE THE SCREEN

Squeeze out as much water as you can. Then pull the top screen off the mixture, and dry it even more with the paper towel.

LET DRY

Remove the bottom screen. Then let the paper dry completely. You will need to make several pieces of paper for the journal.

TIP

It might take awhile for your handmade paper to dry. Try to squeeze as much water as possible out of the mixture, and then put it in a sunny place to dry. You might even need to wait overnight. If the paper is still moist when you move it, it might fall apart.

MAKING THE CD CASE JOURNAL

Once you have the paper started, it's time to make the journal.

REMOVE THE INTERIOR
Use the end of a paintbrush or a pencil and pry the interior out from the clear plastic case.

STAMP THE PAPER
Stamp a wild, colorful design on a piece of colored paper. You can use stamping ink, dye or acrylic paint. Use multiple stamps to make an intricate pattern. For this journal, I chose pink paper, and flowers and swirls stamps.

OUTLINE THE CD CASE
Use the insert, or the front of the CD case, to make an outline on the back of the stamped paper. Outline it twice: for the front and the back of the journal. You can even outline the spine of the CD case so you can completely cover the case with your stamped paper.

CUT OUT THE PAPER
Cut out the outlined CD covers. If you have to, trim the paper again to make sure they fit the front and back of the CD case.

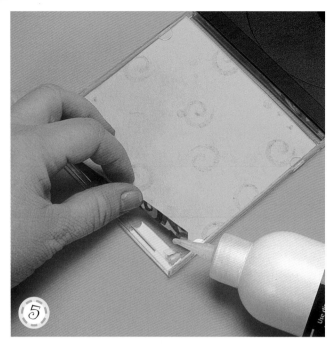

GLUE ON THE COVERS

Glue the front, back and side pieces inside the case. Use just a dot of glue in the corners of each piece of paper. Once the pieces are glued, pop the interior CD piece back into the case.

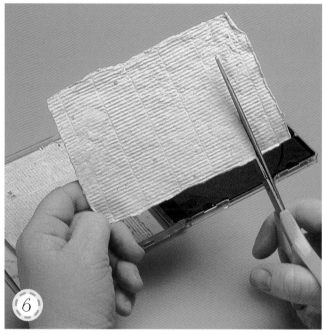

TRIM THE HANDMADE PAPER

Use scissors to trim a piece of the handmade paper so it will fit in the CD case.

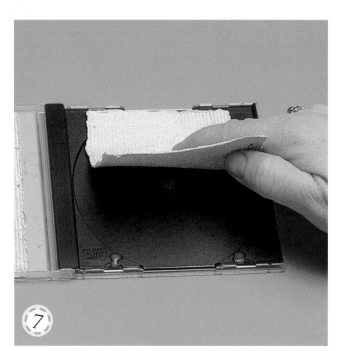

GLUE ON THE HANDMADE PAPER

The handmade paper is for decoration inside the CD case cover. Glue the handmade paper on the inside of the CD case. Use a piece for both the front and back covers.

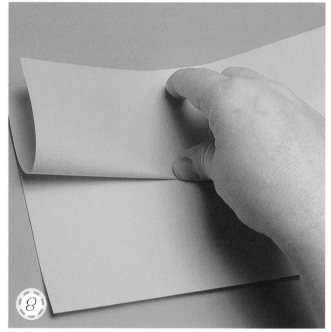

FOLD THE PAPER

Take a sheet of colored construction paper and fold it in half. Then fold the edges back toward the middle on the outside. This is known as a fan fold.

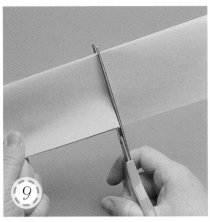

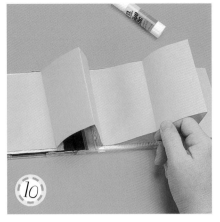

TIP

If you want to add more pages to your journal, just fold and trim another piece of paper. Glue one end of the new paper to the end of the original paper, with the excess hanging to the outside. It should all fold back together when you are ready to close the journal.

CUT THE FOLDED PAPER

Cut the folded paper to fit into the CD case. Cut the top or bottom of the paper, and not along a fold.

GLUE IN THE PAGES

Glue the end pieces of the folded paper to the handmade paper in the CD case.

CHECK THE FOLDS

You should have a fan of paper in the middle of the journal that will fold down when the journal is closed. Close the journal to be sure the paper fits.

ADD A RIBBON

Tie a ribbon around the outside of the CD case to keep it closed.

SILVERY
valentine's day card

Everybody wants a card on Valentine's Day! Can you imagine giving someone special this beautiful card? This is a card you can be proud of, and it's easy to make with just a few stamps and some ink. It's both colorful and cool. With this card, there will be no excuse to give your sweetheart a boring card ever again!

CREATE THE BACKGROUND
Sponge the background of the white card with ink or dye from an inkpad. Use as many colors as you want, in any combination, in bands across the white cardstock. Use different sponges so colors don't mix and turn out muddy.

STAMP THE SWIRLS

Stamp over the sponged area with a swirly stamp using the same ink color as the bands. The image will appear darker because the ink on the stamp is more saturated.

CUT THE CARD

Cut the stamped card in two, across the stamped and sponged surface. Cut enough so your heart stamp will fit in the cut area, and the leftover paper will fit on your card front.

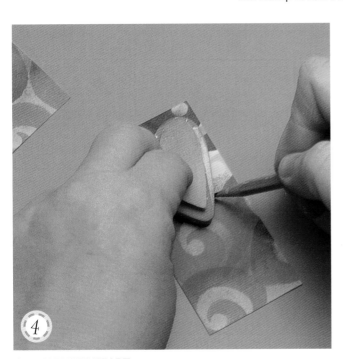

CUT OUT THE HEART

Trace around the heart stamp with a pencil. Then cut the heart out with scissors.

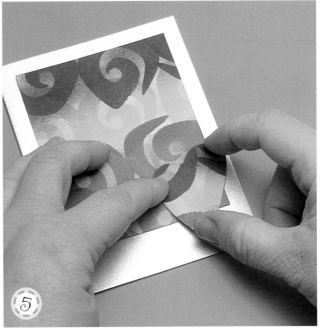

GLUE THE CARD TOGETHER

With a dry glue stick, glue the stamped card centered in the front of a folded silver card. Then glue the heart you just cut out in the corner. For a cool design, make sure the pattern on the heart is different from the stamped card—it will help separate the heart from the background.

treasure
BOX

With a few stamps and a little bit of crafting, you can make any kind of box a treasure box to hold keepsakes, jewelry, secret letters or your favorite collections. With butterflies and the sparkle of mini-mirrors, the box itself is a treasure. Create a bunch of boxes to stack around the room!

Stuff you'll need

- ✓ cigar box or a similar sized box
- ✓ butterfly, leaves, flowers and bugs stamps
- ✓ small piece of thin paper
- ✓ fluorescent green, purple, yellow, pink and aqua acrylic paint
- ✓ gesso
- ✓ assorted size glass pebbles
- ✓ ribbon
- ✓ glitter
- ✓ mosaic mirrored circles
- ✓ scissors
- ✓ highlighter
- ✓ pencil
- ✓ paintbrush
- ✓ clear glaze
- ✓ white glue

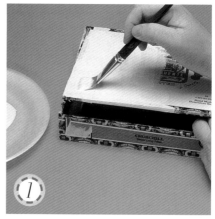

PRIME THE BOX

Prime both the inside and outside of the cigar box. You will need to use at least two coats of gesso. Make sure the first coat is dry before adding another.

TIP

Gesso is a thick, chalky paint used to prime and prepare surfaces for paint. Use it when you want to paint a surface with printing or a picture on it, or when the surface is too slick for paint.

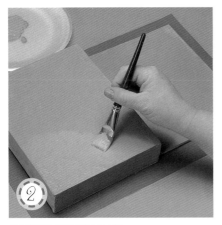

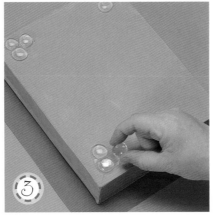

TIP

Glass pebbles can be found at craft stores in the garden section. Mirrored circles can be found in the mosaic section and come in a variety of sizes.

② BASECOAT THE BOX
Paint the cigar box with acrylic fluorescent green. Speckle the paint with short, choppy strokes. It may need several coats.

③ ADD LEGS TO THE BOX
Place a big ball of clear glaze in each corner of the box. Add to the glaze a bunch of glass pebbles as legs.

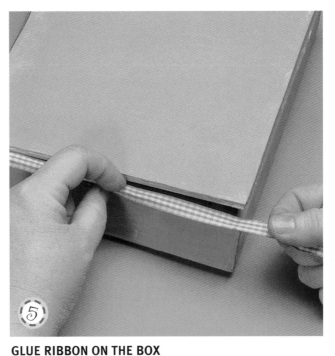

④ ADD GLITTER TO THE LEGS
For extra sparkle, sprinkle some glitter on the clear glaze before it dries.

⑤ GLUE RIBBON ON THE BOX
Use white glue or clear glaze to glue ribbon around the upper edge of the box. Add ribbon over the back hinge of the box, and around the inside lip of the box.

STAMP ON THE LID

Stamp butterflies and leaves on the lid with acrylic paint. Use a different color paint for the wings and body of the butterfly. Stamp on the sides of the box as well. Add painted dots with the eraser tip of a pencil.

GLUE ON THE MIRRORS

Using a clear glaze, add mirrored circles on the top lid and the front of the box.

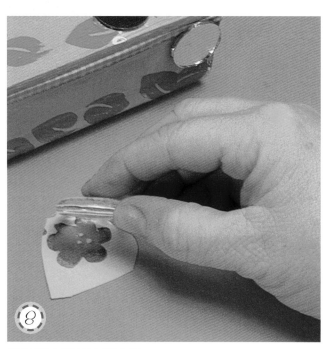

GLUE ON THE PEBBLE

Glue the glass pebble and the stamped image on the treasure box lid. Finish the lid by outlining the images with a highlighter.

STAMP A SMALL IMAGE

On a piece of thin paper, make a single stamp, the size of the large glass pebble. Apply a clear glaze over the image, and then set the large glass pebble on it. Then cut the stamped image and glass pebble from the paper. Cut as close as you can.

MORE IDEAS

You can personalize your box by gluing glass pebbles to pictures of family and friends.

GAME BOX

This box is an excellent gift for a boy you want to do something special for, or for the person you know who loves to play games! Paint the box gold, then add silver and copper swirls to the top. Add dominoes and buttons for decorations. For legs you can use dice. Other game decorations could include bingo sheets on the top, playing pieces glued to the lid and checkers and chess pieces. Old games are cheap and easy to find at yard sales.

MORE IDEAS

Fancy ribbon makes a great border, or trading cards covered in clear glaze is a quick and cool decoration for a card collector treasure box. A celestial box would use stars, moons and suns, while a sport box could have soccer balls, baseballs and a tennis racket.

thank you
caRD

Stuff you'll need

- ✓ handmade paper
- ✓ purple cardstock
- ✓ purple envelope
- ✓ flower stamp
- ✓ purple and green acrylic paint
- ✓ purple ribbon
- ✓ gold gel pen
- ✓ paintbrush
- ✓ bowl of water
- ✓ scissors
- ✓ white glue

This card and envelope are a little tricky to make. They use handmade paper for extra texture and variety. There is some careful stamping and cutting needed here, but the results are gorgeous! This is the perfect card to give as an extra-special thank you and is a work of art all by itself.

STAMP THE FLOWER
On the handmade paper, stamp a flower using green and purple acrylic paint.

TIP

To make this card you will need a piece of handmade paper. You can find directions for making handmade paper on pages 48–50.

OUTLINE THE STAMP
Use the gold gel pen to outline the stamped image.

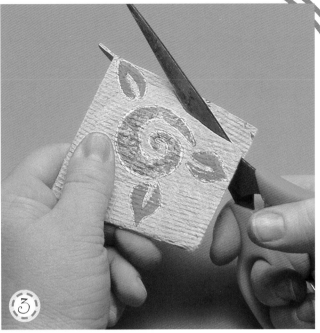

TRIM THE HANDMADE PAPER
Cut around the flower stamp. Leave a ½" (1cm) border around the stamped image.

WET THE PAPER
Wet the edges of the handmade paper with clean water and a paintbrush. Don't get water on the stamp.

PULL THE EDGES
Carefully pull the wet edges of the paper away using your fingers. Don't pull away too much paper. This will give the paper a frayed edge. Let the paper dry.

MORE IDEAS

You can use the basic techniques for this card to make cards for any occasion. Choose stamps with a theme that match the occasion. A change in colors will do much to give each card individuality, while the handmade paper and gel pen will give the card extra flair!

TIP

A nice ribbon and metallic gold outliners can add a touch of class to many projects!

6

FINISH THE CARD
Glue the flower on the corner of the card, then tie a ribbon around the front edge of the card. Tie a bow to hold the ribbon in place.

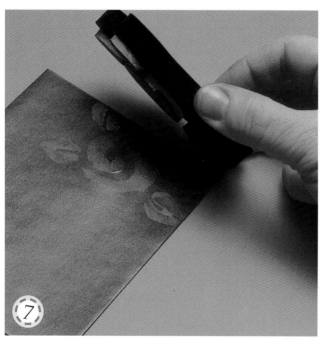

7

STAMP THE ENVELOPE
Stamp the same flower you used before in the corner of the envelope.

8

OUTLINE THE FLOWER
With a gold gel pen, outline the flower on the envelope to match the flower on the handmade paper.

ReSOURCeS

Most of the material and supplies in this book is stuff you can find around the house or at your local stamping or craft store. If you are having trouble finding a particular tool or material, ask someone who works at the craft store or check out the Internet. The companies below are just a few of the many great resources out there for stampers and crafters.

Acey Deucy
P.O. Box 194
Ancram, NY 12502

American Art Stamp
3870 Del Amo Blvd.
Torrance, CA 90503
(310) 371-6593
Fax (310) 371-5545

Fiskars, Inc.
7811 W. Stewart Ave.
Wausau, WI 54401
(800) 950-0203
www.fiskars.com

Hot Potatoes
2805 Columbine Place
Nashville, TN 37204
(615) 269-8002
www.hotpotatoes.com

Judikins
17803 S. Harvard Blvd.
Gardena, CA 90248
(310) 515-1115
www.judikins.com

Marvy-Uchida
3535 Del Amo Blvd.
Torrance, CA 90503
(800) 541-5877
www.uchida.com

MORE FUN CRAFTS
from North Light Books!

Use your favorite rubber stamps to create 25 gorgeous gifts and miniature works of art! Inside you'll find dozens of simple methods for creating sophisticated embellishments on everything from lampshades and pushpins to adorable mini shadow boxes and handmade books.

ISBN 1-58180-081-9, paperback, 128 pages, #31667-K

Use rubber stamps to decorate candles, jewelry, purses, book covers, wall hangings and more. 16 step-by-step projects show you how by using creative techniques, surfaces and embellishments, including metal, beads, embossing powder and clay—even shrink plastic!

ISBN 1-58180-128-9, paperback, 128 pages, #31829-K

Mold polymer clay into a fantasy world right out of your imagination! Maureen Carlson shows you how to sculpt 10 easy shapes that can be used to create dozens of different creatures and characters, including dragons, goblins, fairies, ghosts, pigs, dogs, horses, bunnies and more.

ISBN 1-58180-286-2, paperback, 64 pages, #32161-K

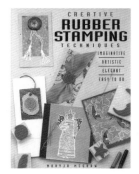

Learn how to create fancier greeting cards, cooler note cards and prettier invitations with MaryJo McGraw's easy-to-master methods. Inside you'll find more than 30 fast, fun, step-by-step projects that mix and match techniques for truly original results!

ISBN 0-89134-878-6, paperback, 128 pages, #31201-K

These and other fun North Light Books are available from your local art & craft retailer, bookstore, online supplier or by calling 1-800-448-0915.